the
BRUCES

by Bill Fyfe Hendrie

Sept names include:

**None other than the ancient spelling
Brus.**

D0682931

the
BRUCES

MOTTO: We have been

PLANT BADGE: Rosemary

TERRITORY: Annandale, Nithsdale, Clackmannan.

Tartan featured on the cover is Ancient Bruce

Published by Lang Syne Publishers Ltd. Clydeway Centre,
45 Finnieston Street, Glasgow G3 8JU
Printed by Thomson Litho, East Kilbride
Design by The Quick Brown Fox Company (Scotland) Limited
© Lang Syne Publishers Ltd. 1997.
I.S.B.N. 185 217 065-4

Reprinted 2007

THE ORIGINS
OF THE
CLAN SYSTEM

by Rennie McOwan

The original Scottish clans of the Highlands and the great families of the Lowlands and Borders were gatherings of families, relatives, allies and neighbours for mutual protection against rivals or invaders.

Scotland experienced invasion from the

Vikings, the Romans and English armies from the south.

The Norman invasion of what is now England also had an influence on land-holding in Scotland. Some of these invaders stayed on and in time became 'Scottish'.

The word clan derives from the Gaelic language term 'clann', meaning children, and it was first used many centuries ago as communities were formed around tribal lands in glens and mountain fastnesses.

The format of clans changed over the centuries, but at its best the chief and his family held the land on behalf of all, like trustees, and the ordinary clansmen and women believed they had a blood relationship with the founder of their clan.

There were two way duties and obligations.

An inadequate chief could be deposed and replaced by someone of greater ability.

Clan people had an immense pride in race.

Their relationship with the chief was like adult children to a father and they had a real dignity.

The concept of clanship is very old and a more feudal notion of authority gradually crept in.

Pictland, for instance, was divided into seven principalities ruled by feudal leaders who were the strongest and most charismatic leaders of their particular groups.

By the 6th century the 'British' kingdoms of Strathclyde, Lothian and Celtic Dalriada (Argyll) had emerged and Scotland, as one nation began to take shape in the time of King Kenneth MacAlpin.

Some chiefs claimed descent from ancient kings which may not have been accurate in every case.

By the 12th and 13th centuries the clans and families were more strongly brought under the central control of Scottish monarchs.

Lands were awarded and administered more and more under royal favour, yet the power of the area clan chiefs was still very great.

The long wars to ensure Scotland's independence against the expansionist ideas of English monarchs extended the influence of some clans and reduced the lands of others.

Those who supported Scotland's greatest king, Robert the Bruce, were awarded the territories of the families who had opposed his claim to the Scottish throne.

In the Scottish Borders country – the notorious Debatable Lands – the great families built up a ferocious reputation for providing warlike men accustomed to raiding into England and occasionally fighting one another.

Chiefs had the power to dispense justice and to confiscate lands and clan warfare produced a society where martial virtues – courage, hardiness, tenacity – were greatly admired.

Gradually the relationship between the clans and the Crown became strained as Scottish monarchs became more orientated to life in the Lowlands and, on occasions, towards England.

The Highland clans spoke a different language, Gaelic, whereas the language of

Lowland Scotland and the court was Scots and in more modern times, English.

Highlands dressed differently, had different customs, and their wild mountain land sometimes seemed almost foreign to people living in the Lowlands.

It must be emphasised that Gaelic culture was very rich and story-telling, poetry, piping, the clarsach (harp) and other music all flourished and were greatly respected.

Highland culture was different from other parts of Scotland but it was not inferior or less sophisticated.

Central Government, whether in Edinburgh or London, sometimes saw the Gaelic clans as a challenge to their authority and some sent expeditions into the Highlands and west to crush the power of the Lords of the Isles.

Nevertheless, when the 18th century Jacobite Risings came along the cause of the Stuarts was mainly supported by Highland clans.

The word Jacobite comes from the Latin for James – Jacobus.

They wanted to restore the exiled Stuarts to the throne of Britain.

The monarchies of Scotland and England became one in 1603 when King James VI of Scotland (1st of England) gained the English throne after Queen Elizabeth died.

The Union of Parliaments of Scotland and England, the Treaty of Union, took place in 1707.

Some Highland clans, of course, and Lowland families opposed the Jacobites and supported the incoming Hanoverians.

After the Jacobite cause finally went down at Culloden in 1746 a kind of ethnic cleansing took place. The power of the chiefs was curtailed.

Tartan and the pipes were banned in law.

Many emigrated, some because they wanted to, some because they were evicted by force.

In addition, many Highlanders left for the cities of the south to seek work.

Many of the clan lands became home to sheep and deer shooting estates.

But the warlike traditions of the clans and

the great Lowland and Border families lived on.

Their descendants fought bravely for freedom in two world wars.

Remember the men from whence you came, says the Gaelic proverb, and to that could be added the role of many heroic women.

The spirit of the clan, of having roots, whether Highland or Lowland, means much to thousands of people.

A map of the Clans Homelands.

CHAPTER ONE:
STAKING CLAIMS

Robert the Bruce

There can be no prouder name in Scottish history than that of Bruce. Yet originally the Bruces were a French family, who came to England as part of the peaceful Norman Conquest of that country. They were granted their first lands in 1101, when King Henry I bestowed the manors of Collingham and Righton in Yorkshire on Robert de Bruis.

Robert was one of five sons of Adam, Lord of Bruis in Normandy, where the remains of the family's stronghold can still be seen at Brix, to the south of Cherbourg. The family estate passed to Adam, the eldest Bruis son, and, as younger brother, Robert therefore came across the Channel to seek his fortune as best he could in England.

It was while he was at the royal court of King Henry that he first encountered the young Scottish Prince David. The two youths got on well and when the prince became King David I of Scotland he remembered his French friend by making him Lord of Annandale in the south west of Scotland.

By the start of the 14th century the French and Yorkshire branches of the Bruce family had died out, but the Bruces of Annandale continued to flourish. As early as 1291, Robert Bruce of Annandale made a bid for title to the throne of Scotland. In that year he became one of the 13 Competitors as the claimants to the Scottish throne became known. His right to the crown was soundly based on the fact that as the eldest son of the daughter of David of Huntingdon, he was the closest relative to King Alexander II, whose son Alexander III died without a direct heir, when he fell from his horse and fell over the cliff onto the rocks near Kinghorn, while riding home to spend the night with his young French bride.

At first it was agreed the Scottish throne

should pass to Princess Margaret, the Little Maid of Norway, but when she died in Orkney on her journey to Scotland the way was left open for Robert Bruce and his rivals to stake their claims.

Bruce along with the other Competitors agreed that King Edward I of England should be the judge of these claims. Edward took a whole year to decide in favour of John Balliol, grandson of the eldest daughter of David of Huntingdon, who was known for his weakness and willingness to be an English puppet. Despite his bitter disappointment, Bruce immediately looked to the future of his family, by announcing that from then on he would champion the right to the throne of his eldest son, Robert. Robert never succeeded in making good that claim, that honour having to wait for his son and namesake.

Robert, son of Bruce the Competitor, married Marjorie, Countess of Carrick. Their first son Robert, the future King of Scotland, was born at Turnberry on the Ayrshire coast in 1274. During his boyhood and youth, he travelled widely, not just visiting his father's estates around Lochmaben in Annandale, Aberdeen-shire and Yorkshire, but also in Kintyre and across the St. George's Channel in Ireland.

When he was eighteen he succeeded his father as Earl of Carrick. He married Isabel of Mar and she bore him a daughter, Marjory, before her death at a young age.

Like his father, Robert refused to acknowledge John Balliol as English puppet king of Scotland, but like his father and most other Scottish lairds did swear loyalty to King Edward. In those days the concept of nationality was less developed.

While his father remained faithful to Edward until his death, Robert declared, "I must be with my own" and joined Sir William Wallace and John Comyn as Guardians of Scotland. In 1302, when Edward offered a truce he accepted it and gave some support to the English king's campaign during the following year.

Bruce remarried, his wife this time being Elizabeth de Burgh. Shortly afterwards, his

Sir William Wallace

Sir William Wallace, braveheart hero, joined Bruce and John Comyn as
Guardians of Scotland.

father died in 1304 and upon inheriting the Bruce estates south of the border, Robert became one of the richest men in England. In spite of all he now possessed, and ran the risk of losing, Robert threw in his lot with the fight for Scottish independence at the beginning of 1306.

In February of that year Robert met his fellow Guardian John de Comyn in the church at Dumfries. In a furious quarrel during which the Comyn refused to support him and apparently threatened to reveal Robert's plans to John Balliol, the Bruce stabbed him to death.

Robert the Bruce challenges Red Comyn.

For committing such a deed in a holy place Bruce was excommunicated by the church, but despite the shame, he gained a great deal of support in Scotland for his claim to the throne. He was crowned at Scone by Isabella, Countess of Buchan. This open act of defiance spurred Edward to send his troops in pursuit of Robert. The Bruce was defeated in attacks at Methven and at Dalry near Tyndrum. Many of his followers, including three of his brothers were caught and executed, but Robert succeeded in making his escape to the Western Isles.

Robert's little daughter Marjory was arrested along with the Countess of Buchan at Tain, where they had sought sanctuary in a holy shrine and was sent by the English to the Tower of London. There she was imprisoned in a small iron cage and forbidden to talk to anyone apart from the Constable of the Tower. She was later sent to a nunnery before being returned to Scotland.

Meanwhile Robert came back from the isles to the mainland where he continued to gather support, marching through the Great Glen, all the way north to Inverness. By 1308 he controlled all castles north of the Forth and gave orders that they be destroyed so that they could not be re-occupied by the English. Gradually his power grew throughout the Lothians and Borders and Linlithgow Palace was regained for him thanks to the wily Farmer Binne, who tricked the English garrison into opening the portcullis gate.

By 1314 Stirling Castle alone remained in English hands defying the Bruce, but instead of attacking and trying to capture it, Bruce's eldest brother Edward, who never grasped the logic of his leader's policy of destroying castles, agreed a one year truce. By this the castle's Governor, Philip de Mowbray promised to surrender unless it was relieved by mid-summer's day 1314. The scene was thus set for the final showdown. King Edward II was forced to march his army north to Stirling's defence and Robert the Bruce to prepare for the battle, which neither leader was really confident that they wanted, but which in the end was to win Scotland's freedom!

CHAPTER TWO:
BANNOCKBURN

On the eve of the Battle of Bannockburn in June 1314, Robert the Bruce and his Scottish soldiers knelt and repeated the Lord's prayer. Seeing the Scots on their knees, King Edward II of England, son of the old Hammer of the Scots, is said to have jeered and declared, "See they are already begging for mercy!" Riding by his side, his esquire De Umfraville replied, "Yes, your majesty, they ask for mercy, but not from you. I tell you these men will not flee for any fear of death".

Bruce and his supporters might well have felt like fleeing, because as they settled for the night on the banks of the Bannock Burn, they must have been able to see that they were very heavily outnumbered, their six thousand infantry and five hundred lightly armed horsemen comparing miserably with the sixteen thousand English infantry and two thousand five hundred cavalry.

Just before darkness fell on that brief June night, Bruce rode out on his pony to review the lines, when suddenly he was confronted by the fully armour clad English knight, Henry De Bohun. As the knight pulled his sword to slay the Scottish king and leave the Scots leaderless for the next day's fray, Bruce hit back with the only weapon he carried, his small battle axe. With one blow he felled his great English adversary and as he rode back amongst his men, his followers deemed his success the best possible omen they could have for the battle, which was to begin at dawn, on June 24.

At first light King Edward began to deploy his troops, but the swollen waters of the Bannock Burn made the job difficult because of the limited space. Looking down from the higher ground to the north, King Robert observed the difficulties which the English were experiencing getting into position. Contrary to his usual practice, the Bruce therefore decided to sacrifice the advantage of the high ground to launch the attack. Swiftly he gave orders for three of his four blocks of infantry to advance and attack, while holding his own infantrymen back in reserve.

The three forward squares of Scottish infantry soon came under heavy attack, but thanks to the homework, which the Bruce had done the previous day, they were spared the worst of attack by the much feared English cavalry. For Bruce had had his men dig knee high ditches and fill them with sharp pointed branches of trees and now the English horsemen found themselves floundering in these watery pits.

The Bruce then sent his own five hundred horsemen forward to disperse the English archers. The flooded Bannock Burn made it difficult for Edward to move up his reinforcements and the situation was made even more congested by his own retreating bowmen.

Now, Bruce judged, was the moment to lead his block of Scottish infantry forward to win the day. Seeing that victory was theirs, even his camp followers left their vantage point on nearby Gillies Hill, waving white sheets. The English mistook them for a further regiment of reinforcements. Taking to their heels, the rout was complete. Many of the Englishmen, who

The clash of sword and spear at Bannockburn.

had survived the fray, died as they fled, falling into the swollen waters of the Bannock Burn, which was said to have turned red with the blood of the vanquished.

Edward and five hundred of his cavalry at first sought refuge in Stirling Castle, but were refused entry by Governor de Mowbray, who realised that he must soon surrender to the Bruce, who when that time came treated him with all honour.

Meanwhile Edward and his nobles rode fast, not stopping until they reached Winchburgh, half way between Linlithgow and Edinburgh, and finally making good their escape by commandeering a small sailing boat at Dunbar and sailing south to England.

CHAPTER THREE:
THE REIGN OF BRUCE

While the Bruce had won the battle, the war against England was far from over and indeed continued for most of his kingship. Cross border raids continued and did much to harry the English troops, but without defeating them.

In 1318 the king was forced to extend his campaign to Ireland to try to rescue his eldest surviving brother, Edward who had been made king of that country three years earlier, but who was being opposed. Despite Scottish reinforcements led by King Robert, Edward was in the end killed at the Battle of Dundalk.

Back in Scotland Robert continued to refuse to recognise letters sent to him by Pope John, addressed to the Guardian of Scotland. In 1320 he met with his fellow Scottish nobles at Arbroath and together they signed the famous declaration proclaiming Scotland a nation in its own right, which they defiantly sent to Rome.

In 1322 King Edward II led his army to

Edinburgh, but Bruce's customary scorched earth policy again won the day and faced with being unable to feed his men, the English monarch was forced to retreat. Five years later his son and successor Edward III's campaign against the Bruce did not even succeed in crossing the border and he was forced at last to negotiate. This resulted in the Treaty of Edinburgh in 1328, which finally recognised Scotland's freedom. It came just in time. Bruce signed it as he lay seriously ill in bed at Holyrood. He was convinced that he was dying of leprosy, a disease that was much feared in Scotland at that time, as can still be seen from the little slanting leper squint windows in several Scottish churches such as Dunkeld Cathedral and Torphichen Preceptory.

Whether or not the Bruce suffered from the dreaded leprosy or not has never been proved, but he was fatally ill. Despite this, he struggled to make a pilgrimage to Whithorn in the south western tip of Scotland. This may in some small measure have made up for his inability to fulfil his lifelong ambition to go on a Crusade to the Holy Land as a penance for his excommunication.

From Whithorn King Robert was carried north to die at his manor at Cardross, between Dumbarton and Helensburgh overlooking the waters of the River Clyde. There on his bed, he decreed that the moment he drew his last breath his heart should be cut out and that it should be carried on the Crusade he had been denied in life by his faithful ally, the Good Sir James Douglas.

His dying wish was honoured and while his body was buried at Dunfermline Abbey in the Kingdom of Fife, Sir James set out with his heart on a Crusade against the Saracen Turks. Sadly he was slain fighting in battle in Spain. According to tradition his final act was to hurl the Bruce's heart in its lead casket before him into the fray.

Afterwards the lead encased heart was retrieved and returned to Scotland where it was buried at Melrose Abbey.

Chapter Four:
The Bruce Line

King Robert Bruce was succeeded in 1329 by his son to his second wife and queen, Elizabeth de Burgh, who became King David II. Although only five years old the little king had already gone through a child marriage the previous year to seven year old Princess Joanna, sister of the English King Edward III in an attempt to secure peace between the two troubled countries.

Young King David was crowned at Scone, a special miniature sceptre being made for him to hold, but his grip on Scotland was less secure. Many of the rival nobles refused to recognise the boy king, favouring instead Edward, son of the late John Balliol. For safety King David and Queen Joanna were taken from Dumbarton Castle on the banks of the River Clyde and smuggled by sea to France, the same route which was to be followed two centuries later by the infant Mary Queen of Scots. Like Mary they spent their childhoods in France before returning to Scotland in 1341.

King David faithfully maintained the auld alliance with France and in 1346 fighting at the Battle of Nevill's Cross he was badly injured and captured by the English. He was kept prisoner for eleven years until in 1357 the Scots agreed to pay a huge ransom for the return of their king. He proved to be a good monarch. Despite the great increase in export and import duties required to pay the annual instalments on his ransom to England, Scottish trade increased. King David tried to give more say in the running of the country to the people, by defying his nobles to summon a Scottish parliament. Sadly his controversial proposal for a union of the crowns was rejected by this very parliament, yet this was exactly what his father the Bruce had tried to engineer through David's childhood marriage to Joanna.

On Joanna's death, David married again, this time to Lady Margaret Drummond or Logie, but he died in 1371 without a legitimate heir.

The Scottish throne then passed to his nephew Robert II, the son of his half sister Marjory and her husband, Walter the Lord

High Steward, thus beginning the royal house of Stewart. The tomb of Marjory Bruce is in Paisley Abbey, where Queen Victoria had a monument erected to her memory and where a stone effigy of the princess may also be seen.

Meanwhile during his life King David had granted his cousin Thomas, the second son of his uncle Edward Bruce and his wife Isabel of Atholl, the lands and barony of Clackmannan on the northern shore of the River Forth between Stirling and Kincardine. On the death of David I, it was to Robert the son of Thomas Bruce of Clackmannan that the role of chief of the family passed.

The Bruce family extended their power to other towns in the Forth Valley, including Airth and Culross in the latter of which they became particularly important.

To this day their mansion is known as The Palace and it was to it that Sir George Bruce welcomed King James VI and 1st in 1617 on his only royal visit to Scotland after his succession to the English throne in 1603.

William Bruce of Clackmannan emigrated

to Russia, where his success may be judged from the fact that his eldest son James was created Count Bruce by the Czar Peter the Great. From this enterprising branch of the family, Bruces established themselves in Scandinavia, Poland and what is now Germany. By the close of the seventeenth century there were members of the Bruce family to be found in America and in the West Indies.

Back at home in Scotland, the Bruce family had achieved high status first in 1663, when the newly crowned King Charles II created Sir Thomas Bruce, Earl of Elgin and again in 1647, when Charles honoured Edward Bruce of Carnock, who was the cousin of Thomas, with the title, Earl of Kincardine. The two titles came together in 1747, when the 4th Earl of Elgin died without a direct male heir and was succeeded by Charles, Earl of Kincardine.

Most famous of all the Bruce family who travelled the world, was however, James Bruce, who was nicknamed the Abyssinian, because of his famous expedition to that country, now Ethiopa, during his search for the source of the

River Nile. Born at Kinnaird House in Stirlingshire in 1730 his "Travels to Discover the Sources of the Nile" was published in 1790, but his adventures were at the time generally considered ficticious thanks mainly to criticism by Dr. Johnson, although later explorers confirmed all that he had written. After such an adventurous life, Bruce died at Kinnaird in 1794, after falling down stairs.

Everyone looked up to the Bruce warriors.

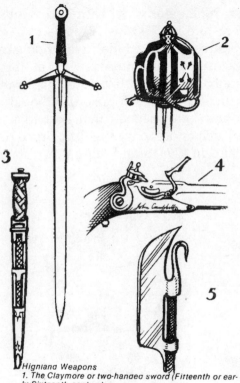

Highland Weapons
1. The Claymore or two-handed sword (Fifteenth or early Sixteenth century)
2. Basket hilt of Broadsword made in Stirling, 1716
3. Highland Dirk — Eighteenth century
4. Steel Pistol (detail) made in Doune
5. Head of Lochaber Axe as carried in the '45 and earlier.